FROM NOW TO 'WOW' IN

CW00869415

Copywrite @ Sylvia Baldock

Printed in the United Kingdom

ISBN 978-1-63068-671-0

FROM NOW TO 'WOW' IN 30 DAYS

Contents:

TIP 1 – THE POWER OF PERSONAL PRESENCE

TIP 2 – WHAT IS UNIQUE AND SPECIAL ABOUT YOU?

TIP 3 – SPENDING MORE TIME IN 'FLOW'

TIP 4 – STAYING IN 'FLOW', A QUICK RE-CAP

TIP 5 – TAKING TIME OUT FOR YOUR HEALTH AND WELL-BEING

TIP 6 – DOING WHAT YOU LOVE

TIP 7 – ESTABLISHING YOUR VISION

TIP 8 – IDENTIFYING YOUR VALUES

TIP 9 – A SENSE OF PURPOSE

TIP 10 – CONFIDENCE

TIP 11 – FIRST IMPRESSIONS, A QUICK RE-CAP

TIP 12 – THE LITTLE THINGS THAT MAKE A BIG DIFFERENCE, A
QUICK RE-CAP

TIP 13 – AUTHENTICITY

TIP 14 – PREPARE FOR SUCCESS

TIP 15 – PREPARE TO GIVE A CLEAR MESSAGE

TIP 16 – BEING 'PRESENT', – A QUICK RE-CAP

TIP 17 – HOW BEING 'PRESENT' MAKES YOU A NETWORKING STAR

TIP 18 – HOW TO PUT ON YOUR HAPPY FACE!

TIP 19 – LEAVE YOUR WORRIES BEHING, BE FULLY PRESENT AND
CONTRIBUTE, A QUICK RE-CAP

TIP 20 – HOW TO BE MEMORABLE, A QUICK RE-CAP

TIP 21 – STAY IN TOUCH THROUGH SOCIAL MEDIA, A QUICK RE-CAP

TIP 22 – USE AUDIO AND VIDEO ON YOUR WEBSITE

TIP 23 – THE POWER OF TESTIMONIALS, A QUICK RE-CAP

TIP 24 – AUDIO AND VIDEO TESTIMONIALS, A QUICK RE-CAP

TIP 25 – GIVING BEFORE YOU RECEIVE

TIP 26 – SUPPORTING OTHER PEOPLE'S EVENTS, A QUICK RE-CAP

TIP 27 – GIVING AWAY VALUE, A QUICK RE-CAP

TIP 28 – WHO DO YOU SPEND YOUR TIME WITH

TIP 29 – INVESTING IN YOU, A QUICK RE-CAP

TIP 30 – YOUR PERSONAL BRANDING STATEMENT

FROM NOW TO 'WOW' IN 30 DAYS

Foreword

This book came about quite by accident!

I was encouraged to give away some free value after hearing Ant Hodges speak at the Business Wealth Club in Oxford. http://www.hodgesnet.co.uk

He talked us through a cycle of steps we could take from creating value to getting it out there to the masses using an incredibly easy App called 'Audioboo'.

I followed his advice, wrote a Blog on my specialist subject – 'Personal Presence', downloaded Audioboo on my iPhone, recorded my Blog and uploaded onto my social media platforms!

Hey presto, I suddenly had my free value out there in the public domain for everyone to listen to.

That was so easy, I decided to record a Top Tip on Personal Presence every day for 30 days.

By the time I reached day 30, I had decided to commission someone to type them all up so I had some good copy to use again in talks, Blogs etc.

I had some editing done and them re-edited the copy myself and added some wonderful quotes to emphasise each tip.

I suddenly found myself with over 20,000 words – in other words – a book!

I have always wanted to write and just never had the time, I told myself I would write when I eventually retired – goodness knows when that will be. I love my work so much that retiring is not on my radar!
So, this is a real gift for me and for anyone who reads it and derives benefit from my thoughts and experience.

It is designed to be a 'Tip a Day' – easy to read and easy to apply.

Ideal for busy people who have a pile of books they just never get round to reading because the chapters are too long and they just don't have enough time to get through them.

One tip will take just a few minutes to read and will finish with a great quote to inspire you throughout the day.

I do realize that even with a short tip very day, there will be some days when you are up at the crack of dawn for breakfast meetings or holidays etc and there is barely time to think never mind read. I have therefore included a quick recap in many of the sections to remind you of the previous tip and to cement the learning.

Some topics have spanned across 2 Tips as I felt they needed more attention, so although they may at first appear similar, they are actually addressing another aspect of the topic.

So why personal presence? I have long been fascinated with people. What makes them tick? What makes certain people more successful than others? Why do some people just stand out from the crowd while others merge into the background?

How can certain people create an instant rapport with strangers while others take several meetings to feel comfortable with new acquaintances?

Having run 9 networking groups for 7 years and taught hundreds of people how to network effectively, I have had a wonderful melting pot of characters to observe and analyse over the years.

Add that to my time as a Nursing Sister in Glasgow, many years ago, where I interacted with people from many varied and bizarre walks of life, and I feel I have great insight into life's rich tapestry of personalities.

I have also attended Personal Branding workshops and read extensively on the subject. My thanks to the wonderful Nikki Owen for her inspired writing in 'An Audience with Charisma' which I have re-read often.

I am a real 'people watcher' and in so doing, I have been able to bring my thoughts together in the following pages to inspire you to follow suite and be the best version of yourself you can possibly be.

My Top Tips are the typical behaviours I have observed in successful people and each and every one of us can apply these tips to our daily life to ensure we stand out from the crowd and are seen, heard, heard of and remembered long after we have left the room. Hence the title – **'From Now to 'WOW' in 30 days'**.

I am now running a series of 'Personal Presence' workshop which are having a dramatic effect on the confidence, self-esteem, clarity and vision of all the attendees.

I am loving every minute of creating and running these powerful days and watching the impact they are having on those who are sharing my journey has been totally inspiring.

I just have to share one testimonial with you –

"I just wanted to write to state my thanks again. Your workshop today was amazing. You really allowed the individual to shine through and created a safe atmosphere in which to share and grow. I think, in the future, I will look upon this day as the first day of the rest of my life. What a truly amazing job to touch people's lives in the way that you do. Many Thanks", J.H.

Enjoy!

TIP 1 – THE POWER OF PERSONAL PRESENCE

"If your presence doesn't make an impact, your absence won't make a difference." Trey Smith

Have you ever walked into a room and just been drawn to someone as if by magnetism? You can't put your finger on it, you just sense that person will be warm, interesting, easy to talk to and engaging.

Equally have you ever been in a room and then watched someone walk in who has an instant impact? People notice them, want to engage with them, hear what they have to say and they move effortlessly around the room spreading their own special kind of 'Magic' wherever they go!

We have all met people with strong Personal Presence – sometimes described as 'Charisma'. They are just 'comfortable in their own skin' They have a quiet self-assurance that makes everyone around them feel at ease too.

This is 'Personal Presence' at it's best and people who have it in abundance, ooze confidence devoid of arrogance, and radiate a feeling of well-being which infiltrates everyone they connect with.

Many people think that 'Personal Presence' is something you are either 'born with' or without and it's true that even babies can exert a strong presence from birth, however, the good news is that **we can all develop a stronger 'Personal Presence' by taking some very simple steps.**

One of the key ways to develop your 'Personal Presence' is to be really clear and assured in your own natural talents and abilities, knowing exactly where you add value and what is unique and special about you.

We are all as unique as a fingerprint, there has never been anyone like us before and there will never be anyone like us again!

Yet, so often, we forget the skills and natural abilities we have as life takes over. Responsibilities weigh heavy on our shoulders and our 'resistance' tells us that we are not good enough or clever enough to be anything other than 'ordinary' and that we should be content to settle for 2nd best!

So many factors influence the person we turn out to be – our background, upbringing, education, friends, career, interests, health, fitness etc – the list is endless and we so often settle for what we are expected to be by parents, teachers, bosses, colleagues, partners, friends and children.
Our true brilliance gets buried beneath those feelings of how we 'should' think, act, behave and simply 'be'

SO HOW CAN WE INCREASE OUR 'PERSONAL PRESENCE'?

This is a huge topic and trainers run week long courses and more in this subject alone so this book just scratches the surface however there are some instant steps that can make a significant difference right now and this book is my **Top Tips to increase your Personal Presence in just 30 days.**

TIP
—
1

My first Tip is to believe that you can develop your Personal Presence to a much higher level and to be assured that it will have a dramatic impact on your business and your life.

I strongly recommend that you engage a personal/business coach who will ensure you keep moving towards your goals and challenge you to reach even higher!

"A strong Personal Presence can be irresistibly attractive, combine it with passion and drive and you will be unstoppable! It will open doors for you, make you stand out from the crowd, get you in front of people you would otherwise never meet, create incredible opportunities and ensure you leave a lasting impact wherever you go".

TIP 2 – WHAT IS UNIQUE AND SPECIAL ABOUT YOU?

Start by writing down the words that best describe you.

Having **key words** that describe your talents, skills and your personality will give you a much clearer picture of how you can '**stand out from the crowd'.**

Strong **personal presence** means you are comfortable in your own skin, you know who you are and you're confident in what you have to offer.

You may not be feeling very confident or special right now, however **you are unique** and it's time to celebrate that uniqueness and share it with the people around you.

So, **how do people describe you**? What words do they use when they are thanking you for a job well done or recommending you to someone else? Do they say how reliable you are, what a great service/product you provide, that you always go above and beyond the call of duty, that you are a pleasure to work with?
If your best friend was describing you to someone, what words would they use?
Would they say you are –
Dependable, friendly, warm, engaging, trustworthy, professional, caring, talented, a great listener, go the extra mile, caring, funny, knowledgeable?
If you were being interviewed for the Press and they really wanted to 'Big' you up, what words could you give them to **show how special you are, what have you done that you are proud of?**

Write down all the key words that best describe you and be bold, this is not a time to be a 'shrinking violet', it is time to identify the words that will show others what's unique and extraordinary about you and which will get you and your business on the map!

If you have 'Post it' notes to hand and a 'Sharpie' or highlighter pen – just write **one word** in bold letters on each 'Post-it 'and then put those words wherever you will see them most. If you don't have 'Post-its', a large sheet of paper will do – just make sure the words are big enough for you to see them at a distance.

The ideal place to display your key words may be on your fridge, office door/wall, by your bed, around your mirror – wherever it is, it is important that you can see them often to **remind yourself of all the unique qualities you already have**. You can add to these words whenever you recognise a new strength or skill you already have or have newly acquired.

If space is tight for you, then photograph your key words and save them as your screensaver on your laptop and phone so you see them every time you logon.

I can assure you, they will be a **great boost to your confidence,** especially when you are having a tough day and need to be uplifted. They can also be used in your marketing, social media, emails and your **'Elevator Pitch'** at networking events.

So be bold, write as many words as you can, if you get stuck, ask a close friend/relative to describe you and capture their words too.

Then put them somewhere visible right away and revisit them often.

"The hardest challenge is to be yourself in a world
where everyone is trying to make you be somebody else."
Poet, E. E. Cummings

| TIP ─── 2 | Take time out today to contemplate and re-discover the special qualities that are unique about you. Write down the key words that best describe you and keep them visible every day. |

TIP 3 – SPENDING MORE TIME IN 'FLOW'

'FLOW' is the natural unfolding of our lives into wholeness and harmony.

When you are in 'Flow', you experience a feeling of energized focus and you are totally aligned with the task in hand. You are absorbed, focused and the day just whizzes by. At the end of it you feel energized rather than drained and you have a deep feeling of satisfaction in a day well spent and a job well done.

I am afraid that most of us spend so much time doing the tasks that we feel we 'have to do' or 'should do' to keep our businesses and life on track, that we lose sight of where our heart lies, our natural talents, the things we love to do and are inspired by.

We add most value to our life and our business when we are fully in **'Flow'**, the motivation and inspiration come naturally, we see brilliant results for our efforts because we are using our natural talents to do what we do best. Business and life becomes a joy rather than 'hard work' or a 'struggle'.

SO HOW CAN YOU SPEND MORE TIME IN 'FLOW'?

Take a little time now to just close your eyes and think of times when you have been **fully in 'Flow'** in the past:- What were you doing? Where were you?

If you were with people:-
Who were they?
What were they saying?
How were you feeling?

If you were alone:-
What were your surroundings like?
What were you saying to yourself?
How did you feel?

Get yourself back into that situation in your minds eye –
You might have been working with a client and they were thrilled with what you did for them.
You might have been training, coaching or mentoring others and they had major breakthroughs as a result.
You might have been writing a really impactful article.
You may have been delivering an important presentation that you prepared well for and delivered much better than you expected.

Whatever the situation, if you can **recapture it in your mind and feel some of those feelings again, it will really help you to define your 'in Flow' times.**
Capture 2 or 3 situations when you have been really in **'Flow'** describe them as fully as possible in writing, then compare them and write down the common factors in each, so you can easily **identify when you are most in 'Flow' and how to spend more of your time in 'Flow'**

So how much of your time are you in **'Flow'** in your daily working life right now? How much time do you spend doing those tasks that you are naturally proficient in and energized by? – the tasks that come easily to you, that inspire and engage you and that you do really well?

Think about what you have been doing in the past few days – how much of the time was spent fully in **'Flow'**?

Identify ways in which you can be more in **'Flow'** every day, **when you are in 'Flow' you positively 'Glow' and people who 'Glow' have a strong Personal Presence!**

"I've come to believe that each of us has a personal calling that's as unique as a fingerprint – and that the best way to succeed is to discover what you love and then find a way to offer it to others in the form of service, working hard, and also allowing the energy of the universe to lead you". Oprah Winfrey

TIP 4 – STAYING IN 'FLOW', A QUICK RE-CAP

'FLOW' is the natural unfolding of our lives into wholeness and harmony.

Being in 'Flow' gives a wonderful feeling of energised focus as we use our natural talents to do what we do best. We are totally aligned with the task in hand, time flies by and at the end of the day we feel energised rather than tired.

The more time we spend in **'Flow'** the stronger our **Personal Presence** becomes.

So let's take a look at what takes you **out of 'Flow'**?

Do you have tasks that are frequently on the bottom of your 'to do' list, very often go on next day's 'to do' list, and then get transferred to next week's and sometimes next month's?

These are the tasks you don't enjoy – in fact, that you often dread doing. So you put them off, and they niggle away at the back of your mind, draining your energy.

When you at last get round to doing them, you are **not** engaged, you are **not** enjoying them, you are **not** energised by them.

You are **out of 'Flow'**.

When you are out of **'Flow'**, your **personal presence** is much lower.

In the space below, I'd like you to write down a list of those things you do in your business, which take you **out of 'Flow'**.

List all the activities on your 'to do' list that you really don't enjoy and you are not very good at. Be completely honest. Write down the tasks you dislike and put off, which keep you from getting on with what you are naturally brilliant at and where you can add the most value.

So what can you do about those draining tasks that are taking you **out of 'Flow'**?

Believe it or not, there are people out there who actually **love** those tasks you don't like doing, who sail through what you struggle with. You can find them online, through social media and at networking groups, a wonderful opportunity to meet people with the skills and expertise you need.

You don't need to 'employ' them which incurs the necessity of contracts and PAYE. You can simply **engage them for the number of hours it takes them to do those tasks** that take you out of **'Flow'**

Even better, when you offload tasks that drain your energy and take you away from what you do best, you **allow other people to be in 'Flow'**.

I can hear you saying: *"I can't afford to delegate, I need to make my business more profitable. That is my priority."*

Unfortunately, many business owners think they have to make loads of money before they can offload the tasks that drain their time and energy.

But guess what happens? They find they don't grow or flourish as they'd hoped. They are just too bogged down in endless 'To Do' lists.

By offloading even just a couple of hours of the tasks you don't do well, you can **reinvest** your precious time and energy into:

- Planning the **growth** of your business;
- Prospecting for **new clients**;
- Most importantly of all, **doing the work you excel at**, which adds the most value to your business and secures your future success.

You will find you're spending **much more time in** '**Flow**', and you will have that **added energy**, that **wonderful glow** and a **stronger personal presence** that makes you stand out from the crowd and attracts people to you who want to work with you even though they may not know why!

"We all have natural gifts. We all have a purpose. Imagine how it would feel to align those gifts with their purpose. Would that make a difference? So many people travel though their lives waiting for the 'right moment', or that 'something' that will transform their world ... when all along it was waiting for them ... inside".

TIP 5 – TAKING TIME OUT FOR YOUR HEALTH AND WELL-BEING

*Do you **value** the person you are enough to allow yourself time to rejuvenate, refresh **and recharge your batteries?***

People with a **strong personal presence** often glow with health. You can tell just by looking at them that they look after and value themselves.

However, it's easy to lose that 'glow' if you're not careful. Ambitious, motivated and goal-oriented people are always busy people. If you have a demanding job or if you run your own business, you can find yourself working long hours at the expense of your own wellbeing.

It's all too easy to put yourself at the bottom of the 'to do' list. All of the things that make you feel better get pushed further down, or off the list altogether.

These activities are so important. Often they only take a short time, and are easy to slot into a busy day – for example:

- Moving away from your desk to reflect or meditate for 5-10 minutes.
- A short walk in the sunshine
- Sitting and reading an inspirational book for just 10-15 minutes

It can also be time to simply relax and not think about anything at all. By switching off, you allow your brain to recover from the stresses of a busy week and the pressures of work. By taking time out, even for a short time, you can then start to work more creatively.

I'm sure you will have found, when you take time out, especially in the fresh air on a beautiful day, you get back to your desk and you are actually far more productive and far more creative.

So how can you build in some **'me time'** every single day?

It doesn't need to be an hour at the gym, pushing yourself to the limit. It can be a 10-15 minute walk around the block, allowing your brain to **relax, refresh and rejuvenate**, so that when you get back in front of that laptop you are composed, relaxed and ready to tackle the challenges of the afternoon.

By giving yourself the gift of 'time out', you **value yourself** more. You will begin to realise that **YOU** are your most precious asset and, by caring for yourself properly, you will gain a higher self-esteem.

So, get off that treadmill and get into the habit of scheduling precious time in your diary just for you.

Value your biggest asset. Look after yourself effectively, so that you are working at your peak performance every day. People who look after themselves and have health and wellbeing at the forefront of their minds, operate far more efficiently.

They have that wonderful 'glow' of wellbeing. When you **'glow' with wellbeing** you have a much **stronger personal presence**.

"The most adventurous journey to embark on; is the journey to yourself, the most exciting thing to discover; is who you really are, the most treasured pieces that you can find; are all the pieces of you, the most special portrait you can recognize; is the portrait of your soul." C. JoyBell C

TIP 6 – DOING WHAT YOU LOVE

It is so important to take time out of your busy schedule, to do whatever you like to do.

But what would be best for you? What energises you and helps you to value yourself more?

Some people are energised and also relaxed by an extreme workout, pushing themselves and getting those endorphins flooding around their bodies. Afterwards, they feel motivated and focused.

Others are drawn to commune with nature. They enjoy getting out in the lovely fresh air and it relaxes them to take the time to appreciate the changes in nature and the scenery and to drink it all in.

I'm a Pisces. I love being near water, and am very fortunate to live near a reservoir and a canal. Just getting close to it and hearing the sound of it flowing, makes me feel at peace.

I know some people who find a bike ride the perfect way to take time out. It could be a gentle ride through the woods, or the enjoyment of pushing up those hills, feeling the muscles straining and enjoying the challenge.

Singing is a great 'feel good' activity. I know several people who have joined a choir because it makes them feel good to be part of a group of people that have one purpose. Singing together with others is really energising, floods you with serotonin and makes you feel joyful. So, it might be that you choose to join a local choir and sing your heart out.

If you have a busy work life, which is overly stimulating and you are surrounded by people most of the time, then time alone may rejuvenate you. That might be in the form of meditation, just taking time out to be quiet, to empty your mind and let it recharge, to just slow down and simply 'be'.

We are so often humans **'doing'** rather than humans **'being'**.

When was the last time you listened to your favourite music?
Really listened to it? I mean lying back on the sofa soaking it in, not just having it as background noise. If you love music, if it motivates and inspires you, then why not take some time out to enjoy it fully.

Do you have a pile of books beside your bed that you mean to read
but never quite get round to?
Just 5 or 10 minutes out of your busy day to read some pages from one of those inspirational books will energise you, focus you, and give you that wonderful feeling that of learning and growing.
I have got favourite books that I dip into frequently, that constantly inspire and motivate me. I love to read inspiring words last thing at night and first thing in the morning – they shape my nights and my days.

Most importantly, how much quality time do you spend with those who are dear to you?
It is so wonderful to spend time with your family, with your friends, people that you value and people who really value you – re-connecting, laughing together, sharing food. What better 'feel good' factor could there be, and yet for some who do not value their wellbeing, that quality time with others gets put to the bottom of the list.

'Variety is the spice of life', so **make sure you have a good mix of things in your life that make you feel good**, so that you are not just working, working, working and never reaping the benefits and rewards of your labour.

We are not meant to be working 'all the hours God sends', we are meant to have **balance** in our lives and one way to achieve this is to have that quality **'me time'** every day.

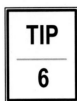

TIP

6

When you allow yourself that quality time, you will feel good about yourself, you will recognise that you are an extremely valuable asset and you will dramatically raise your self-esteem.

And when you have got **high self-esteem** of course, that raises your **personal presence**.

"Nourishing yourself in a way that helps you blossom in the direction you want to go is attainable, and you are worth the effort."
Deborah Day

TIP 7 – ESTABLISHING YOUR VISION

People with strong personal presence have a really clear vision.
They know exactly where they're going, and what they want to achieve
in their life.
Everything they do is focussed on following that vision and achieving
their goals and their dreams.

When was the last time you sat down and thought about **your vision**?
I would really urge you today to take some time out and think about where
you are going with your business and your life, what exactly you want to
achieve, what is your purpose.

What really thrills you? What skills and talents do you have that will make
a significant difference to the people around you?

To be clear about your vision, it is important to **write it down** and have
it somewhere where you can keep referring back to it.
By doing this you can check that you are not wasting your time and energy
doing things that are not in line with your vision, you can make sure that
everything you do, is moving you towards achieving your goals.

Your Vision Statement should have:-

- **Your primary goal**
-
- **Where you want to be in the future**
-
- **A level of excitement**

You can write your vision statement here.

....

....

....

....

....

....

....

When you write about your vision, think about how you are feeling.
If you don't feel inspired and 'fired up' then perhaps your vision isn't
big enough. It may be time to re-assess where you are going.

We are all changing and evolving all the time and it is very easy to keep
going towards one vision without thinking about the fact that we have
changed and that we may have a new direction in life. So check in with
yourself regularly and **check that your vision is still right for you**.

Every week when you look back at what you have done, assess whether the
things that you have done, the steps you have taken, the ways you have
moved forward, are actually moving you towards that vision and the life you
want to be living in the future.

More and more, individuals and companies have a real sense of purpose.
That sense of purpose is vital as the driving force behind them and their
business.

You have probably heard of CSR, Corporate Social Responsibility.
Many companies now want to be seen to be giving back to the community.
Many business leaders want to leave a legacy and make their mark on
the world.

So what mark are you going to leave on the world? **What difference are
you going to make**?

Take some time out today to think about that big picture, to get real clarity on your vision and to create a **'Vision Statement'** that will keep you on track to achieving the life of your dreams.

Without a vision you can't plan the journey. With a strong vision, you will have a strong sense of purpose. With a **strong sense of purpose**, you will have a far **stronger personal presence**.

"The more boundless your vision, the more real you are."
Deepak Chopra, Life After Death: The Burden of Proof

"Not all dreamers are winners, but all winners are dreamers. Your dream is the key to your future. The Bible says that, "without a vision (dream), people perish." You need a dream, if you're going to succeed in anything you do." Mark Gorman

TIP 8 – IDENTIFYING YOUR VALUES

Very closely aligned with your vision are your 'Values'.

Values are the principles we live our life by. They are the things that are really important to us, sometimes known as the standards, moral principles or ethics we hold dear.

These values guide the way we live our lives and the decisions we make. Personal values are our core beliefs, values, and philosophies that we hold about life, its purpose, and our own purpose. As we grow up, we take on board the personal values of others around us until we reach the teen years and start to accept or reject such values as being a part of who we are, or not a part of our own selves.
Instead of just accepting those values that were ingrained in us by parents, teachers, and society, we need to stop, take a deep look at ourselves, pinpoint our values, and implement them into our lives.

TIP ———— **8**	**Think about what your values are right now.** What are the things that really matter to you? **When you are working, what do you need to hold true?** What would you never compromise on?

I have a great need to make a difference and some of my values include **empowering** others, **inspiring** others and also **'walking my talk'**.
I need to be **authentic**, not just delivering great training but actually living it.
Integrity, honesty and **spirituality** are also really important to me.

What about you? What really makes **you feel good about what you do**? What is important to you? It might be **spirituality,** or **caring** for others, or **trust,** or **self-development** – whatever your values are, it is important to take stock of them regularly and then you can measure everything you do on how it aligns with those values.

Use the space below to write down a list of your values on the left hand side. Then along the top write various headings of the main activities you do in your life.

(You may prefer to do this on an A4 sheet of paper To give you more space.)

For example you might be a trainer and also have coaching, mentoring, workshops and public speaking as your activities.

....

....

....

....

....

....

....

....

....

Now check your activities in with your values. Rate them on a 0, 1, 2, 3, 4 basis, rating as 4 those that are most closely aligned with your values and as 0 those which are not at all aligned.

This activity might surprise you, it certainly surprised me when I did it.
I found that some of the things that I do which I thought were way up at the top of my list, were actually not serving my values as much as others.

This is a great way to plan out how you are going to spend your time, because **you want to be spending most of your time doing the things that really tick all those 'high value' boxes**. These are the things that really serve your purpose, that make you feel that you are being very **authentic** and you are **living the life that you want to live**.
This exercise is incredibly enlightening and it will help you to spend more of your time doing what you're naturally talented at. Think about how much time you're spending working in those **'high value'** areas.

When you are spending more time in those high value areas, I guarantee you will be **much more in 'Flow'**. When you are in **'Flow',** you will have a wonderful inner **'glow'** and of course, you have a much **stronger personal presence**.

"It's not hard to make decisions when you know what your values are." Roy Disney

"Achievement of your happiness is the only moral purpose of your life and that happiness, not pain or mindless self-indulgence, is the proof of your moral integrity, since it is the proof and the result of your loyalty to the achievement of your values."
Ayn Rand (1905-1982); Writer, Philosopher

TIP 9 – A SENSE OF PURPOSE

It is so important to understand your vision and purpose in life,
and to spend most of your time on activities aligned with your values.

If you are doing this, you will have a great **sense of purpose** and you will be really comfortable in your own skin.

What are you doing today? What are your main tasks? You may be meeting with clients, or talking with them on the phone. You may be going out to a networking event, or delivering a presentation, a workshop or some training. You may be spending several hours on a creative project.

Whatever you are doing, it is important to have a strong sense of purpose for that task. This means that you need to be **clear on the outcome** you want **for you**, and the outcome you want **for your clients or prospects**.

Having a strong sense of purpose will give you a real air of **confidence**, – confidence that you know exactly what you are doing and clarity on what you are aiming for.

In turn, this will give anyone you meet, confidence in you and your ability. Space. People with a real sense of purpose, **inner confidence**, clearly defined vision and values are constantly progressing because they **know absolutely what they are all about** and where they are going.

When you meet these people, who are moving towards their vision, you can see those changes. Every time you meet them, they have progressed in some way. It may be small changes at first, but every little step moves them forward until you see them take some big leaps and end up exactly where they want to be.

You can make sure you **keep your sense of purpose strong**. It's very simple.

Always make sure you take a few minutes to:- **define your purpose for your actions or interactions** before you:-

- Go into a meeting;
- Pick up the phone;
- Write a report;
- Take part in a brainstorming session;
- Go to a networking event;
- Create marketing materials

Write down what you want to achieve. If you have that **strong sense of purpose** clear in your mind, then guess what happens? – **You are much more likely to achieve it.**

All too often we just go into meetings, or into interactions with people hoping that we will open our mouth and something good will come out.

If you have prepared for it, if you know **exactly what you want to achieve**, then you are going to be **much more successful**.

It doesn't take long, just a few minutes of your time to get that clarity on your purpose for everything that you do.

This will give you real direction, much greater confidence and will in turn, give others much greater confidence in you.
Confidence has a massive impact on personal presence!

"If you have felt hopeless, hold on! Wonderful changes are going to happen in your life as you begin to live it on purpose."

"Knowing your purpose gives meaning to your life."
"Great opportunities may come once in a lifetime, but small opportunities surround us every day."
Rick Warren, The Purpose Driven Life: What on Earth Am I Here for?

TIP 10 – CONFIDENCE

Imagine somebody with a strong personal presence walking into a room. They appear so confident. They look 'comfortable in their own skin', they have a sense of purpose and move round the room effortlessly.

When they speak, people listen to them. When they walk into that room people want to talk to them and are interested in what they have to say.

What are some of things you can do to **raise your confidence levels**? How can you make sure that when you are at an event or with clients, people see you as being confident and self-assured? How can you project the sort of confidence that will make people listen to whatever you say and want to know more about what you have to offer?

Vision, value and goals are so important here.

If you have a **clear goal**, you can craft a message around that goal. This is so much more powerful than simply giving general information about your business.

If you are delivering a quick 'elevator pitch', it is important that you are **clear about your purpose,** confident about what you have got to offer, and you have a clearly defined **'call to action'**.

In networking groups, people are keen to hear how they can connect you, and help you move forward in your business.

So if you have a very clear 'call to action', it is so much easier for them to help you. Say something like "today I am looking for ..." or "my call to action is...."
With a clear 'call to action' you are far more likely to get the **results** you want.

Showing that you have **prepared,** makes you look professional. People are far more likely to want to work with you because you are showing you are somebody who puts effort into what you do rather than just pitching up and 'winging' it on the day.

Preparation is vital in order to raise your confidence levels and raise your **personal presence**. Prepare well for those 1-2-1 interactions, on the phone or face to face. Take time to think about what your **specific goal** is for that interaction, what is the best outcome for you and for the person you are talking to.

Writing your goal down means that you can be very clear about the steps you need to take to make your interactions as productive as possible. If your goal is to go away from that meeting with some specific actions and decisions made, you will be much more likely to direct the conversation to achieve your outcomes.

Our time is really precious, and all too often we waste time through lack of direction, lack of purpose and lack of goals.

TIP

10

Planning ahead with your vision, values and goals in mind will make you feel more **confident**, more **effective**, more **professional** and will of course, greatly **increase your personal presence**.

"It's not what you say out of your mouth that determines your life, it's what you whisper to yourself that has the most power!" Robert T. Kiosaki.

"What the mind can conceive and believe, and the heart desire, you can achieve." Norman Vincent Peale

TIP 11 – FIRST IMPRESSIONS, A QUICK RE-CAP

There is no better investment than good preparation.

The time spent defining your purpose and goal before you make a phone call or go to a meeting, pays dividends. You will be clear about the desired outcome, so you will say the right things and follow the right plan of action. You then end with the result that works best for you and best for your prospect or your client.

There is another important area where preparation is paramount – your **image**.

ARE YOU CREATING THE RIGHT FIRST IMPRESSION?

Like it or not, we all make judgements on people the minute they walk into a room. Our subconscious brain absorbs all the external information about that person, processing it and deciding what it means.

As soon we meet someone, we are processing what they are wearing, how clean their shoes are, what their hair looks like, what their body language is like and so on. All of that information builds up a picture of that person in our minds and our important first judgement happens instantly – **within the first few split seconds** of somebody walking into a room.

You may say "I don't want to be around people who judge me before I speak!" But I must stress that people are not **consciously** judging you. It is a subconscious process that the brain goes through of subliminally absorbing and assimilating all the information from the external 'you'.

Whether we like it or not, **image matters**. It is important to think about the external impression you give as soon as you walk into a room, and to plan your appearance in advance.

I've seen people turn up at networking events looking like they got dressed in the dark or looking like they have just walked the dog and come straight to the networking event. I know they may be trying to look casual, however it doesn't make a great professional first impression. If you are in a room full of people who are looking for someone to network with, **they are going to network with people who care how they look, who look like they have invested some time in preparing for the event**.

When we see someone who looks like they haven't taken any time over their appearance, subliminally we are thinking –
> *"Well if that's the care they take with their appearance, then that's probably the care they take with their work".*

Already you are giving the impression of some, or all, of the following –
Little attention to detail
Lack of planning,
Possibly low standards on delivery
Probably miss deadlines.

So - "no thanks!"
So why set yourself up to fall at the first hurdle?

Get some really good advice on your **colours and your style**. I run eight networking groups and I have seen women join my groups who are lacking in self-esteem and lacking in knowledge of how to dress professionally. They just don't look the part for networking events and client meetings.

However, as soon as they take advice on their colour and style, they come back looking amazing, wearing colours and styles that suit them. They are wearing make-up in the right colours for them, and they look smart and professional.

Everybody always says something like – 'Wow, you look amazing!'. Imagine the impact that has on their confidence?
They stand straighter, **they walk taller**, they look **more confident**. When they stand up to deliver their 'elevator' pitch, they deliver it much more confidently and as a result, people then want to meet with them afterwards.

The whole impact of looking good and feeling good is massive. It makes you look professional, ensures **you stand out from the crowd** and **gets you noticed and remembered.**

Colour is also incredibly important. I love to wear bright colours and every time I do, people come and talk to me and compliment me on the colour. They remember me because I stand out from the crowd and look different. It makes me feel great because I love colour, it energises me and really enriches my life.

Get a little bit bolder with those colours! If you haven't had your colours done, please take the time to see an image style consultant, it is a worthwhile investment in your future, it's a knowledge you'll then have for life and which will pay dividends for years to come.

It is just as applicable for men as it is for women – wearing suits, shirts and ties in the right colour and cut will **greatly enhance your image, your confidence and your personal presence**. I refer more to this in the next Chapter.

This investment in yourself will also save you a fortune. When you shop, you will know exactly what colours and styles suit you, so you'll save time and money – no more of those costly mistakes.
Who wants a wardrobe full of clothes they don't wear because they don't feel good in them? It is true that most of us wear 20% of our wardrobe 80% of the time!

Invest in an **Image and Style Consultation**. Being **confident** and **feeling good in what you wear** gives you a much **stronger personal presence** and you will love the way it makes you feel!

TIP

11

"Appearance matters a great deal because you can often tell a lot about people by looking at how they present themselves."

Lemony Snicket, The Miserable Mill

"Your appearance, attitude, and confidence define you as a person. A professional, well-dressed golfer, like a businessperson, gives the impression that he thinks that the golf course and/or workplace and the people there are important."

Lorii Myers, Targeting Success, Develop the Right Business Attitude to be Successful in the Workplace

TIP 12 – THE LITTLE THINGS THAT MAKE A BIG DIFFERENCE, A QUICK RE-CAP

Making an impactful first impression is so important, I can't repeat it enough. When you walk into a room what is it that people notice about you first? What are those subliminal judgements people are making about you based on the way that you look? Appearance, is such a huge subject, that I would like to address some aspects of it in more detail.

My advice to invest in an **image and style consultant** is not just aimed at women, but also at men. There are many things which men can do about their external appearance which will make them look **more professional, sharper, more at the cutting edge of what they are doing and which will make them stand out from the crowd.**

Far too many men network in suits that have seen better days, which have not been made to measure, which no longer fit particularly well. Their shirts are faded, their ties have become slightly dated. There's so much you can do to improve the way you look and make that **vital first impression**.

So, for both men and women, investing in appearance is an investment in your future. Understanding how to look your best and how to be appropriately dressed for each occasion is a **skill for life**. Much of the way you look is to do with the way you feel. Nurturing yourself, eating well, getting enough sleep and taking quality 'time out' will all make you look and feel better.

Being well groomed is also really important to enhance your **personal presence.** Take your hair for example, it does not cost much to have a decent haircut. It's never a good idea to take the quick, cheap and easy route of getting your partner to do it (unless they are a hairdresser). Investing in a good hairdresser who will cut your hair in a style that suits you will pay dividends in making you look younger, more professional and up to date. If you colour your hair, then get colours that suit you – many hairdressers now study colour and can advise you on a colour that suits your skin tone and your eyes. The impact is quite remarkable! Once you have your **professional haircut**, make sure it is always **clean and well styled** when you are networking and meeting clients. Your hair is one of the first things that people notice.

For women, there is the issue of make-up. Turning up wearing no make-up at all can look as if you haven't taken much time or care over getting ready. You may be a lady who doesn't like wearing much make-up. However, you don't need to wear it heavily. Just a little bit of definition around your eyes, a little bit of lipstick or lip gloss, will accentuate your natural features and make you look more professional and better prepared for the occasion. It's about **enhancing what you've got**, not masking your natural attributes.

Both men and women need to take care of their skin. Make sure your skin is **well moisturised**, because if you are looking healthy and your skin looks good, then you are putting out the message that you are in control of your life, you are taking care of yourself, inside and out.

Nails need to be well groomed. This is one of my big bugbears. I went to a conference in London, a really big conference, a three-day event, a couple of years ago. I met up with an image consultant colleague of mine, who asked if she could tag along. She was wearing bright blue nail varnish, which was badly chipped. She was very conscious of it all weekend and it looked awful! There was nowhere around for her to get any nail varnish remover or do anything about it. This is the perfect example of a **tiny little thing** which **gave a really bad impression**.

Certainly, if I had been meeting her for the first time, I wouldn't have chosen her as an image consultant because she turned up with nails that looked anything but professional. A small detail ruined her all-important **first impression** and first impressions count!

I went to another conference run by a very successful entrepreneur. I was really looking forward to hearing him speak and was sitting in the front row. He came on stage wearing shoes that looked like they'd been worn for 2 years without ever being cleaned. I spent the first few minutes transfixed by his shoes and although what he said was very impactful, he lost some authenticity on his appearance.

So, **little things make a huge difference**. Really think about your appearance, it's not just about the clothes that you wear, it's also about:
- How clean you look
- Your hair
- The way you're made up
- The texture of your skin
- Having clean, well groomed nails
- Having clean shoes.

All of this makes up a bigger picture of someone who **takes time over their appearance and who cares about how they look**.

Those subliminal messages are being absorbed, – if we take care of how we look then we will probably pay great attention to the quality of the work that we deliver and the services that we offer. In people's mind it's all incredibly closely linked.

Turning up to a meeting or event, wearing whatever you fancy that day, making little or no effort and taking the 'like me as I am' attitude, is like trying to run a marathon with heavy weights on your back. Why start a relationship by giving a poor first impression and then have to work really hard to be accepted as a professional business person?

TIP 12

People remember the way you looked the first time they met you, long after the event.
Make looking after **YOU** a priority and adopt the habit of looking good for every occasion. The result will be that you will feel **so much better** about you, you will know you look your best, you will network more confidently, you'll relate to your clients with more assertiveness and your **personal presence** will be much stronger.

"You never get a second chance to make a first impression, so make sure the first impression of you is the best version of yourself you can possibly muster"

Tip 13 – AUTHENTICITY

Do you 'walk your talk'? Authenticity is so important in creating the right impression with people who want to work with you, your clients, your prospects, your colleagues.

I WANT TO START BY TELLING YOU A STORY.

I was at the Professional Speakers Conference in London. It was an important event, there were about 140 delegates. I had been looking forward to it for a while, I had a great new outfit to wear, a bright yellow dress, a little jacket that went really well with the dress and a scarf that pulled all the colours together.

I felt **really good** as I walked into the event, and the first thing that was said to me as I was met by the organiser was 'Wow, you look **fantastic!**' Well, you can imagine how that made me feel. That happened to me several times throughout the day. I had strangers saying to me – 'I love what you are wearing', people coming up to me, introducing themselves and saying – 'I love your colours'. It really **got me noticed**.

Now one of the questions that you are asked most when you network with speakers is, 'what do you speak about?'. So of course my answer to that question was '**Personal Presence'!** It was so congruent with what I was wearing, several people said 'ah, hence the outfit' and they really connected my passion for personal presence with the colourful outfit that I was wearing. That's really important, because when I re-connect with them, they will remember me as the 'girl with the yellow dress who talks about **personal presence'** because they have already made that connection in their mind.

So I am being **authentic**, I am **walking my talk**.
For me, dressing to impress gave me great **confidence**, I was very at ease networking, I met some great people and I had a really good day.

So, my question to you today is, **what can you do to show that you walk your talk, what can you do to show that you are authentic?**

Let me give you some examples.

If you are a web designer for example, is your website absolutely fantastic? Are you directing people to it? Are they 'wowed' by it? Are you constantly updating it with the latest technology? Have you got video content on there, audio content, are you showing people what you can do for them? If you are a web designer and people are thinking of using you, that's the first thing they are going to look at.

If you are a graphic designer, do your business cards, your flyers and your promotional material have the 'wow' factor? Do people look at them and think 'wow, what a great designer!'?
Do the visuals leave a lasting impact on their mind, the sort of impact that will make them want to work with you?

Perhaps you are something less visual, an accountant or a bookkeeper for example, and you are thinking: "How can I show my authenticity?"
Well, a bookkeeper from one of my networking groups, stood up and said "I know exactly how much profit I am making today, and I know that every day". That's pretty impressive, not many of us could say that. She was really showing that she **walks her talk**.

If you are a solicitor and you've got some really great success stories, where you have gone above and beyond the call of duty, then use them. Use them in your 60 second elevator pitch, use them in your marketing materials and on your website.

TIP	Establish your **authenticity**, walk your talk! This will make you stand head and shoulders above people who offer exactly the same services or products as you do,
13	but who don't know how to demonstrate their authenticity.

Write down in the space below some of the ways in which you are unique and special, some of the ways in which you stand out from fellow competitors who offer very similar services to what you are offering.

....

....

....

....

....

How do you stand out? How can you get that message of that uniqueness out to the people who are looking at and considering, working with you. How can you get it into your 60 seconds, or your elevator pitch, into conversations with prospects and onto your website?

One great way to establish your authenticity is to have some very current testimonials on your website, on your blog, across all social media. We have so many great mediums now to get testimonials out there. Do use those stories wherever you can.

With authenticity comes **confidence** and with both of those qualities comes a much **stronger personal presence**.

"This above all: To thine own self be true, And it must follow, as the night the day, Thou canst not then be false to any man".
Hamlet, Shakespeare

We need to find the courage to say NO to the things and people that are not serving us if we want to rediscover ourselves and live our lives with authenticity. Barbara de Angelis

TIP 14 – PREPARE FOR SUCCESS

I would like to look a little bit deeper into preparation. Preparation for events, for meetings with clients and prospects, and for networking.

Preparation should always include gaining more knowledge around our specialist subject because being **confident** about what you're talking about and having **new knowledge** to share will get you noticed and position you as an 'authority' in your field.

So when you are going into a meeting or going to an event, just think about the type of people you are going to be meeting and what sort of information you think they would be interested in.

Nowadays, we are so fortunate to have Google at our fingertips, we can Google anything and glean more information about it.

Whatever your specialist subject or whatever you may be promoting at that meeting or event, do a little more research, do a little background reading.

Make it your goal to come up with **two or three new pieces of information**, results of research, new statistics that you can inject into your conversations with the people you meet at the event, or your clients or prospects that you've got that 1-2-1 meeting with.

What this does is it positions you as an '**expert' in your field**. People love to learn and if you can help them to learn by sharing a new piece of knowledge, then they will see you as a very useful connection.

Not only that, **sharing new information** will help you feel more confident. You will have something new to talk about at networking events and something interesting to refer to when you are in those interactions with your clients and your prospects.

In marketing, the word **'new'** is almost as impactful as the word 'free', so the more **new information** you can bring to your conversations, the more knowledgeable you will appear and the more people will want to get to know you better.

Do you do your people research before networking events? This might seem very basic, but too many people go to networking events without doing any research into the people they are going to be meeting or the companies they are going to be connecting with.

If you are planning to introduce yourself to certain people at networking events (and this is often made very easy as you receive guest lists in advance), then you can **research those guest lists**, decide who you want to meet with and research them in advance.

Set the scene for Success
Research people before you meet them. Check out their websites, Google them and study their 'LinkedIn' profiles and testimonials. Connect with them on social media and send a 'looking forward to meeting you' message.

TIP 14

How much more professional do you look when you can have an informed conversation with somebody because you have **researched** them? You know what they are all about, what they are aiming for, you know what their company values are and you've got a really good feel for their organisation.

Equally, if you are going into a client meeting, you look incredibly professional when you have done your research into their background, their interests and when you have read some of the things their clients say about them.

Of course, looking and feeling **professional** will make you feel much more **confident**. With confidence comes that increased **Personal Presence**.

Talent alone won't make you a success. Neither will being in the right place at the right time, unless you are ready. The most important question is: 'Are your ready?' Johnny Carson

TIP 15 – PREPARE TO GIVE A CLEAR MESSAGE

I was at a breakfast recently, and at that meeting I was looking around the room and taking note of people who had a strong personal presence.

Those people stood up and delivered their 40 seconds with **passion** and **conviction** and by giving a really **clear message**.

Because they knew **exactly what they were looking for**, they came across much more **confidently**. It was obvious that they had thought about what their **purpose** for being there was, they'd prepared their **message** and they knew exactly what they wanted to **achieve**.

Your **40 or 60 seconds in the spotlight** at a networking event is often the only snapshot people get of you. You never get a chance to talk to everybody. So when you stand up, open your mouth and talk about your business, that is the **single impression** that you will make on many of the people there.

HOW MUCH TIME DO YOU SPEND PREPARING YOUR MESSAGE FOR NETWORKING EVENTS?

Do you actually have a **goal** for every single event you go to? Do you know what you want to **achieve**? Do you know what **connections** you are looking for? Without that goal, how can you possible create a really impactful message that will bring the results you are looking for?

My suggestion is to take some time before every networking event, preferably the day before or even a couple of days before and sit down and think about what you really want to achieve from that meeting.

With that goal in mind, **craft your message** so you can achieve what you want to achieve.
Don't make the mistake of trying to cram in a long list of everything you do, but instead pick on something you do exceptionally well and talk about it

with **passion**. Passion is incredibly contagious and it is very difficult not to listen to and pay attention to someone who is passionate about what they are talking about.

So stand up and deliver your 60 seconds, or 40 seconds, with as much passion as you can muster, and make sure you have got a **really clear call to action**. A reminder - It should sound something like "so today I am looking for ..." or "my call to action today is ...." – people at networking events are **inherently invested in supporting you**, in helping you to get the connections that you want to get.

It gives us all great pleasure to give the right connections for somebody and to see that turn into a very successful piece of business. So **make it easy for everybody**. Also, when people are talking about you afterwards, remembering you, it is important that they are very clear about what it is you offer, what is unique and special about you and what you are looking for.

Take time prior to every networking event to set your intention and create a powerful message, with your goal in mind. Include a very clear call to action, that others will understand and use the words you would like them to use when describing you to others.

Standing up and delivering your message with **all the passion about your business you possess,** will ensure that you are **seen**, **heard** and **remembered** long after the event and of course, will give you a much **stronger Personal Presence**.

Enjoy the many benefits that delivering that **goal-focused, passionate and structured message** will bring.

"If you want to accomplish the goals of your life, you have to begin with the clarity".

TIP 16 – BEING 'PRESENT', A QUICK RE-CAP

We've looked at preparing for meetings and events, planning who you want to talk to and doing your research on those people in advance. This will ensure you can start by asking well informed questions about them and their business, which will make you look really professional.

I have emphasised how important it is to do the same when you go into client meetings, doing your **background research** so you know what that client is all about, their values, their aims, their business goals, their ideal clients etc. You can then start that conversation with an impressive level of knowledge which will ensure the best possible outcome.

There is something else that goes hand in hand with preparation, also very important for success, – being '**present**'.

I am sure that many of you have been at a meeting or at a networking event where you have been talking to somebody you have only just met. You ask them some intelligent questions about themselves and their business. They talk for quite a long time about themselves, and then give you a cursory "So, what do you do?"

As you reply, you sense they are not listening to you, or they're looking over your shoulder, watching who is coming in. Now that they've off-loaded what they do, they really want to move on and meet someone else who they can 'sell' to.

Just remember how that made you feel, it didn't exactly make you feel valued did it? Did you feel warm towards that person and want to get in touch with them again? So, be very aware of, **being present** and **listening fully** to the people you are interacting with.

Now somebody who is a master of this is **Bill Clinton**. If you put aside all his failings – what people say about him is that when you are in his presence, you feel like **you are the only person that matters**. He absolutely holds you with his eye contact, he listens 100%, and you really feel that he is **genuinely interested** in you. When he moves away, you feel the loss of his presence.

That's a great gift to have, that when you are interacting with people, they really feel that you care about them, you are interested in them, listening to every word and not only that, you are also absorbing what they are saying.

So how can we be **more present**?
It's hugely tied into **preparation**. Let's recap –

Being well prepared through:-
- Having a clear goal for the event/meeting
- Doing some research into the latest developments in your own area of expertise and into the backgrounds of the people you are going to meet
- Being fully prepared on your 'elevator' pitch
- Knowing your response to the question "What do you do?"
- Getting there early
- Looking your best -if you know you look good you will be much more confident and your **Personal Presence** will shine through.

If you have all of that taken care of, then you will not be wasting brain space worrying about what to say. This means that you can relax and **listen fully** to the people you meet.

If you are **well prepared** in this way and you **feel confident** that you are also looking good, then you are going to be much **more present** at that event.

So really think about how you can be more **present**, and focus on it the next time you meet people. When you are asking them questions, focus on listening 100%, because by doing that, you can then ask the **right questions** and get to that next level of information, that will enable you to **help** that person and to build that **wonderful rapport**.
Building rapport is the basis of all successful networking, it is the starting block for people wanting to work with you and refer you to others.

It also ensures that you are remembered as someone who 'gives' before they receive. People who 'give' first are always the ones who stand out from the crowd.

Practise being more '**present**' wherever you are. Soon it will become like second nature to you and it will ensure you are **seen**, **heard** and **heard of**.

"People may not remember what you do, they may not remember what you say, they will always remember how you made the feel"
Maya Angelou

TIP 17 – HOW BEING 'PRESENT' MAKES YOU A NETWORKING STAR

I want to re-enforce the importance of being present and of really engaging with people rather than just thinking about when you can get your chance to speak and what you are going to ask them next.

I was at one of my networking lunches recently and I was observing the people in the room. I was noticing which of the people there were really **present**.
I recognised them because they were the ones who were listening 100% while other people delivered their 60 second 'elevator' pitch.

I would call these people **networking stars**.

They were taking note of what others were looking for, what connections they were requesting, they were **fully engaged** in the meeting.

When we did an exercise where we were sharing with each other the kind of connections that would really make a difference to us, these people were again really **paying attention**, **taking notes** and **understanding** the needs of others. They were genuinely keen to help everyone, and were coming up with names of people they could connect them to.

When it came to the last section of the meeting, which is called 'Let's Talk Business', they were able to stand up and offer names of connections that would help other people in the room. Now that made them look **so genuine**, it really showed that they were there to 'give' rather than just to 'get', it greatly increased their standing on that **Personal Presence** score.

What happened as a result is that people wanted then to have a 1-2-1 with them, people **wanted to help them in return**.

People who are 'present' and listening fully, are the most successful in networking circles because **they totally understand that networking is all about giving before you receive**.

By being **fully present**, they **understand the needs** of their fellow networkers and they are then able to give. They derive great pleasure out of giving because it is so **rewarding** when you find an ideal connection for somebody else.

At the next meeting, people stand up and they thank them for getting that connection, so again that raises their standing within the group, it **raises their 'presence' within the group**.

Whatever you are doing, be totally present and **in the moment**. You can't change the past, you can't decide the future, the only thing you can change is the moment right now.

So be totally present today, make sure whoever you are with, you are **listening fully**. Focus on ways in which you can help them and connect them to relevant contacts and enjoy that warm feeling that giving wholeheartedly always brings.

TIP 17

Commit to being **totally present 100%** in the **'NOW'** and to **giving before you receive**. You will find that greatly adds to your confidence, your self esteem, your professional standing and of course, your **Personal Presence**.

"Don't live in the past – you've already been there. And don't live in the future, either. Tomorrow will be here soon enough. Live in this moment now – it is sacred and unrepeatable. This moment alone holds valuable gifts that should not be missed." Steve Goodier

TIP 18 – PUT ON YOUR HAPPY FACE!

We have been addressing the importance of being totally present when listening to others and the importance of giving them 100% of your attention. This means quietening the incessant 'mind chatter' we all get and not thinking about what you are going to say or when you are going to get a chance to speak, or what question you are going to ask next.

You should be focusing totally on them and really listening, people are rarely listened to with such generosity and when it happens, they get a sense of being quite special because you are giving your valuable time to listen fully to them.

Building on that 'others first' approach, I would like to talk about **managing your state** when you are going out to a client meeting or networking event.

Most of us have got lots of 'stuff' going on in our lives, some worse than others. We might be going through a particularly **tough time** with our business, cash flow may be really tight, **business might be slow** to materialise.

We might be having a tough time at home, relationship problems or fractious teenagers who are being impossible to manage.

We might have somebody very close to us who has been diagnosed with an illness.

There is all sorts of 'stuff' going on for everyone all the time, but it is really important not to bring that out with you when you are going to an event, like a workshop, networking event or client meeting.

I run several networking groups and I remember in one of my groups particularly, having a member, who I'd greet every month as normal by asking "How are you?" She would then **download everything that was**

wrong with her life, her business and her staff, and I could just feel the energy draining out of me as we spoke.

She was the same with everyone else who asked how she was – she seemed to have this unconscious need to focus on everything negative and to share that negativity with anyone who would listen.

Fortunately, she eventually left the group but it has stuck in my mind how draining that person was and when I am training others how to network effectively, I always use that example.

Everybody has got 'stuff' going on and for a lot of people, particularly single business owners, when they come out to network, it's the only time they get to connect with a community, to get inspiration and training, and they want to go away feeling uplifted and motivated.

If we **all** brought all of our problems to the meetings, people would go away feeling drained and uninspired. We all feel so much better when we have spent time with inspirational people.

There are 2 types of people in this world –'Drains' and 'Radiators' – my advice is the ditch the 'Drains' and surround yourself with 'Radiators' who will inspire, challenge and motivate you to greater success.

" Inspirational people drink at their wells of inspiration daily".
Nick Williams

So one way to manage your state before networking is to **think every day of 3 things that you are really grateful for**.

It might be as simple as having a roof over your head when there are millions of homeless in the world, or having food in the fridge when there are so many starving people in the world, or just having someone who loves you.

Whatever it is, **think of 3 things you are grateful for every morning**. Keep them to the front of your mind, so you can manage the negative stuff that's going on and keep it at bay when you are out there.

Put on your happy face regardless of what's going on underneath. People love to talk to people who are happy. Think about the good things that are going on for you and share those instead. Make every interaction **positive** and **upbeat** regardless of how you are feeling inside.

When you are happy, you radiate joy, you light up the room, other people want to bask in your sunshine and **you leave them feeling better off for being in your presence**.

So in the words of that lovely old British song:-

"Pack up your troubles in your old kit bag and smile, smile, smile".

TIP 19 – LEAVE YOUR WORRIES BEHIND, BE FULLY PRESENT AND CONTRIBUTE, A QUICK RE-CAP

We've looked at being present, fully engaging with people when you meet them for 1-2-1 meetings or at a networking event. We've looked at leaving your worries at home, putting on your happy face and going out and spreading joy around you rather than doom and gloom.

I want to emphasise this point a little further –

You can only be absolutely 'in the moment' if you leave your troubles and worries behind. Only then can you be fully engrossed in what's happening, listening to people around you but also listening to speakers **fully** at events you go to.

Now these events might be conferences, workshops or networking meetings. Whatever the event, you can only make the most of the opportunities presenting themselves by being **fully engaged** with what's going on.

So if life is particularly difficult and you have several issues going on – commit to leaving them at home for the day. There is nothing you can do about them during the event, so compartmentalise them to be dealt with later and **be fully present** in the 'Now'.

Enjoy interacting with everyone you meet. Share the good things about you and your business – focusing on them will lift your spirits and put you in a much more positive frame of mind.

Really listen to the speakers, notice when they pause and want to make a point and takes notes of key points. Show you are fully engaged.

Participate when they ask for input from the audience or ask the audience a question.

All too often, when speakers ask for questions, there is a stony silence and for a speaker that can be really quite difficult to handle.
I always think, if you are going to an event, **put as much as you can into it** because, like everything in life, the more you put into it, the more you get out of it.

So if you are going to a weekend conference for example, do some research on your speakers, read up on the subject, glean some extra knowledge before you get there. Be prepared to contribute – you will get so much more out of the event than if you simply pitch up ready to absorb like a sponge.

BE READY TO ASK QUESTIONS AND SHOW YOU ARE FULLY ENGAGED.

If you find that quite nerve-racking, if you're quite shy and nervous about having your voice heard amongst other people, then my top tip is to **sit at the front of the room** because when you are sitting at the front, you are completely engaged with the speaker.

When you are at the front of the room, you can't see all those people behind you and it's 10 times easier to interact with the speaker or conference leader and to ask questions.
Also, once you have done that several times at various events, it will come much more easily, you will **feel part of the event** and you will stand out from the crowd and **get noticed**.

Now I'm not suggesting for a minute you become one of those annoying people who go to those events and completely monopolise the speaker. They also completely monopolise the floor and actually just want to keep everybody listening to them – that's really going over the top.

However, do make your presence felt by **asking questions**, **answering questions** and by **preparing well** so you not only get the most out of that event, you are also giving back which, in turn, will ensure you are seen, heard and heard of.

TIP 19

Be totally present and prepared for events. By being fully engaged and giving back, people will want to connect with you and get to know you better which will make it a much more fruitful and impactful event for you.

Your **Personal Presence** will be enhanced and you will be remembered long after the event.

"The future belongs to the one most fully alive in the present."

Paul Palnik, Eternaloons: The Palnik Anthology

TIP 20 – HOW TO BE MEMORABLE, A QUICK RE-CAP

We have been talking about the importance of being totally present in your interactions with other people, of fully listening to people, being really engaged, being absolutely present in the moment and also about leaving your worries and problems at home and not bringing them out with you, putting on that happy face and really enlightening people's days.

As much as possible, it's great to add to people's days, rather than detracting by being a drain on their energy.

For today's tip, I would like to talk about the importance of **remaining in people's minds after you have met them**.
This is very much about being **in touch**, **following up** immediately after a networking event, or client meeting.

When we meet people at events or have a meeting with clients, we usually make some sort of **commitment**. We may promise to connect them to someone we know or to send them a piece of information, or to invite them to an event.
Make sure you keep those promises and action them as soon as you possibly can.
I've often been on the receiving end of such promises of connections, information, referrals etc., only to be disappointed with hearing nothing at all. People all too often don't follow up, which is really disappointing and doesn't leave a great impression.

So when I'm teaching people how to network, I always say when you are planning an event or client meeting, **always book some time with yourself in your diary afterwards so you can follow up effectively.**

You can use that time to:
- send the information you promised;
- invite them to an event you talked about;
- introduce them by email to the contacts that would really help them in their business.

When you do that, when you **follow up on your promises**, it is seriously impressive.

This happened to me recently, I met several people at a weekend event and I followed up immediately. One of the guys came back to me straightaway and said "Wow, I am so impressed with the speed of your follow up!"

What I did was I sent him a profile test, (I provide Talent Dynamics profiling). He took the test, and now he's been in touch and we are going to meet up the next time I'm in his area. We have connected in LinkedIn and the relationship is developing.

So that **speedy follow up** is vital to growing those relationships and taking them to that next level. It makes you look **incredibly professional**, it **raises your personal presence** in people's eyes and in their memories and when a situation arises when your services would be appropriate, you will be at the **top of their list**.

TIP
___
20

Set aside time in your diary to follow up after every meeting or event.Professional and speedy follow-up will **accentuate your personal presence** and **keep you high on people's minds**.

What are you doing today to stay in the minds of the people you met last week, last month, last year?

Remember – 'Out of sight, out of mind'.

TIP 21 – STAY IN TOUCH THROUGH SOCIAL MEDIA, A QUICK RE-CAP

We've covered the importance of following up, when you have met someone at a networking event, a conference or when you have had a 1-2-1 or a client meeting.
Taking time out to follow up professionally and as soon as possible, while you are still in their mind, is invaluable.

What builds on following up, is of course, **staying in touch**. It is all very well following up immediately, however, how are you staying in touch? If you are not in regular contact, the valuable time that you have invested with that person just dissipates.

So it's really important to stay in touch, and one of the best ways to stay in touch is of course to **connect on Social Media**. Follow the person you have met on **Twitter**, connect with them on **Linked In**.

LinkedIn is a powerful platform for business connections.

It is a wonderful place for you to **update your profile regularly** so people can see how you are growing and developing and what you are currently offering. They can also see the most recent recommendations you get from clients.

In turn, you can **check other people out** and find out much more about their contacts, their background, their skills and recommendations. You can bring so much more to the conversation. Also connect with them on **Facebook**, add them as a friend, like their page, show that you are not just one dimensional, that you are really getting to know them on all levels.

It is really important that you are **active on social media**. Of course none of us can be active on all the platforms that are out there right now, so it's important to pick the ones that really work for you. That might be **LinkedIn**,

Facebook and **Twitter**, or you might like to use **Pinterest, Instagram,** or **YouTube.** Select two or three that work for you best, and focus on **being on there regularly, adding value,** making sure your **personal presence** is strong across those social media where you are represented.

Think of what you can add in terms of value, your **top tips on your specialist subject, articles of interest** that you have seen, **motivational quotes or pictures** that are constantly being uploaded to Facebook and that we can share so easily. Share **top videos** on YouTube that you have helped you, inspired you, or given you a nugget of **new knowledge.**

There are so many ways nowadays that we can be present even when we are absent. Thanks to social media we can **constantly be on people's minds** even though we are not physically with them or in front of them.

TIP 21

Make sure you are active across all media so that each time people hear from you it just **reinforces that initial 'Wow!' factor** and builds up this **stronger and stronger personal presence** that you have in that person's mind.

It's fun, and soon it becomes a habit. It might seem at first to be quite daunting, but actually once you get into the habit of going onto **Hoot Suite** (for example) in the morning, and adding a quote or an article, it becomes second nature. You can spread that out across all your media and schedule it so you have lots of little touches going on throughout the day.

"Success comes from taking the initiative and following up... persisting... keeping in contact, sharing knowledge, ideas and connections. What simple action could you take today to produce a new momentum toward success in your life?"

TIP 22 – USE AUDIO AND VIDEO ON YOUR WEBSITE

We've examined the use of using social media to build on the connections you make and to develop deeper, more productive relationships.

I would now like to ask you to think about your **personal presence on your website**. Does your website reflect the real 'YOU'? Does it express your passion, your expertise, your uniqueness? Can people sense the 'essence' of you when they are on your site and does it make them want to stay and find out more?

How often do you update your website? Are you keeping it fresh? Adding new information that will attract your ideal client? Are you appealing to people who like to gain information through different media?

Many people are getting **'text tired'**. They just don't have time to read reams of text. The temptation for all of us is to write far too much blurb on our websites, and of course, people only stay on our site for a matter of seconds unless we can really grab their attention.

So think about introducing some **audio**. The tool I used to create these 'Top Tips' is **'Audioboo'** – a free download on your iPhone which is incredibly user-friendly. You can instantly upload anything you have recorded onto any media that you want. So I really suggest trying out 'Audioboo' and sharing your top tips on your specialist subject.

Also, take time to create some **video**. There is **nothing like video for really getting a feel for what a person is like**, and again, it's a media that people like to look at. Many people are visual, so it's much easier for them to watch you on video than it is to read all the text that you have created.

So, aim to have a variety of ways in which people can get to know you on your website.

With video, making sure that it is professionally shot is important.

There is nothing wrong with doing a couple of minutes of quick video on your iPhone to upload to Facebook, or something that you just want to do an instant promotion on. However, for something that is going to be on your website **permanently**, it's really important to get it professionally done. There are many videographers out there on the networking scene who don't charge the earth and it looks so much better than a home shot movie.

Having **professional video on your website** helps people to get a feel for your passion for your business, your expertise and **how professional you are**.

I always check people out on video when I'm meeting them for the first time after connecting on social media. I find a video gives me more insight into what that person is like, how passionate they are, what their area of expertise is and how well they talk about it.

TIP

22

Do invest some time in creating audio or video to create a **stronger, personal presence that is visible online, visible when you are asleep,** and that is available 24/7 for anyone to dip into and find out more about you and what makes you tick.

"What others see in you now is just a MILD chapter of you; the WILD version of your brand is yet to be visible. Just dare to be more visible and the real you will show up!" Israelmore Ayivor

TIP 23 – THE POWER OF TESTIMONIALS, A QUICK RE-CAP

I've recommended that you can establish a powerful presence on your website by taking it beyond just text.

Video is a wonderful way to enhance your personal presence. There is no better way to get to know somebody, (apart from face to face of course) than watching them on a video. You can get a real feel for their expertise in their subject, what they sound like, how passionate they are about what they do and by the time you get to meet them, you almost feel like you know them, because you have seen them in action.

Something else that is incredibly powerful is **testimonials**. Where are your testimonials? Do you ask for testimonials when you have done a great job for someone, or when you have run a brilliant workshop, or delivered really impactful coaching? Once you have those testimonials, do you just file them away somewhere or do you actually **use them** across several different media?

When I am checking someone out, testimonials and recommendations are one of the first things I look for. I'll go onto their **LinkedIn** profile, read a bit about their background, and then I will scroll down immediately to their **recommendations** because I want to see what other people are saying about them.

Do you have recommendations on your Linked In profile? Are they recent ones or are they going back years ago? Testimonials from years ago don't carry the same authenticity as a recommendation that was written last week, or last month.

We are all changing and evolving all the time and we are constantly offering new content, new services, new products. It's important that we have **up-to-**

date feedback on our latest offerings so that prospects can go and read recommendations from people we have worked with recently and get a real feeling of "Yes, this is someone I want to work with!"

So make it a habit to ask for those recommendations. I know sometimes we feel everyone is so busy, we don't want to give them something more to do. However, it's **reciprocal**, when somebody gives you a recommendation on **LinkedIn**, you are then automatically asked to reciprocate. How lovely to do that, it means we are all building up those wonderful testimonials, which are so powerful and greatly add to our authenticity.

Regarding the written testimonials, the ones you get through on email or on a feedback form, what are you doing with them? Do you include a testimonial on the bottom of your emails, or in the body of your emails when you are prospecting, when you're promoting your services or an event?

TIP
___
23

A testimonial really adds **authenticity** to your message. They should be clearly visible **on your website**, your **social media** and **emails** not tucked away in the corner or at the bottom bar of a page that people rarely go to.

Have testimonials scattered throughout your website so that people can see what others think about you. **What other people say about you is infinitely more powerful than what you say about yourself** and will greatly augment your **personal presence** across all media and ensure you stand out from the crowd in your business community.

Also, make sure you have some on the wall of your office and **read them regularly. It's easy to forget what people have said about us** and being able to just look up from your desk and read a glowing testimonial, especially when you are having a tough day, will lift your spirits and make you feel far more confident in your own abilities.

When you are confident, **your personal presence is much stronger**.

TIP 24 – AUDIO AND VIDEO TESTIMONIALS, A QUICK RE-CAP

I have been addressing the power of testimonials and how important it is to ask for testimonials when you have been working with somebody, when you have done a really good job, or provided them with a great service or exceptional new products.

It is at this point, when they are most happy with what you've delivered to them, that is the perfect time to ask for a testimonial. Don't be shy, or reluctant about it. **People are happy to talk about the good things we have provided for them.**

With testimonials, it doesn't just have to be the written word.

Audio is also a wonderful medium. I have already mentioned 'Audioboo', a free download and the easiest possible tool to use. You just press record, you speak, you pause it, you publish it and you share it across all sorts of social media. It couldn't be simpler than that.

So instead of asking someone to write, why not ask someone to speak? Ideally, they could do both, but for some people speaking is easier than writing.

The lovely thing about having **an audio testimonial** is you can add it to your website, share it on Facebook and listeners can actually **hear the passion** in other people's voices when they are talking about you.

Another excellent medium is a '**sound cloud**'. I have worked with Pippa Sawyer, from **Curly Radio** https://soundcloud.com/curly-radio Pippa creates wonderful 'sound clouds' – audio coverage about you and your business. https://www.linkedin.com/in/philippasawyer

She has the perfect voice, exactly like a BBC Radio Two presenter's voice. She introduces you and what you are offering and then she interviews you and other people on your behalf, and creates your '**sound cloud**' which can be added to your website, social media and various marketing platforms.

One of the greatest mediums for testimonials is **video**. Most of us now have iPhones or some sort of phone where we can take video. So why not, at the end of your interaction with your client, ask them if they would mind recording a couple of minutes on video about the service, the product or whatever it is that you have delivered to them?

That is **incredibly powerful** because we get to see that person, talking about you and your services with real sincerity.
For people who are 'text tired', watching a video testimonial for a couple of minutes is a perfect solution and really gives them a sense of what's unique about you and how appreciative your client is.

Remember - What others say about you is infinitely more powerful than what you say about yourself.
 I think sometimes we are put off using audio and video because we think we need to be incredibly technical, we think we need to have all the latest quality equipment.

If you are putting a video on your website that's going to be there forever, then, as previously mentioned, it is important to have that professionally done. However, **the technology we have through our iPhones is perfect for taking testimonials either by audio or video** and the quality is good enough to be used across **all media** and makes your message come alive. It also shows that you are up to speed with technology and that you are prepared to invest your time in reaching your target audience.
It gets you and **your presence** out there across many different media.

So have some fun just experimenting with your testimonials through different media, getting them out there, drawing attention to you through many different channels.

Use Audio and Video Testimonials across all your media. Make use of the wonderful technology at your fingertips and once you've used it once or twice, it will become second nature.

TIP

24

"What other people say about you is infinitely more powerful than anything you will ever say about yourself"

Tip 25 – GIVING BEFORE YOU RECEIVE

I would like to re-enforce the importance of giving before you receive.

If you know people who are very charismatic and have that strong personal presence, you may also recognise that most of them are frequently **giving to other people**.

They just seem to do it naturally and seamlessly. They are in a room, perhaps at a networking event, and just seem to know people that will help the people that they are talking to.

I have been running an exercise with my networking groups where we have been identifying **who would really make a difference** to our business and what connections we would love to make. We have been sharing that with the rest of the group. We have also spent time thinking about which of our connections could be helpful to others.

The **impact** of this has been really quite dramatic. We have been thinking outside the box and introducing each other to connections we have that we know will really help the other person, we have been **giving before we receive**.

The result of that is of course that when you give, and you **freely give**, not expecting anything in return, **people actually want to give back**. That old law of reciprocity just kicks in and people bend over backwards to also find connections for you. That's not the reason why we do it but that's just what happens. You then feel part of a really **supportive network of contacts** who are inherently invested in helping each other to succeed.

So having this attitude of **'giving first'** is a wonderful mind-set to have and some of the many benefits are that you are **seen** and **remembered**, and people will talk about how **effective** and how **giving** you are.

That **raises your personal presence** and your professional standing in the wider network of connections you are known by.

So, when you are going to events, **be really present**, listen to what people are looking for and spend some time thinking about how you can help other people, such as picking up the phone, making a call to somebody and **creating an introduction** for one of your network connections.

We can also give in many other ways. If people are launching a new business, there are ways in which we can help them. There is advice we can give them if they are branching out in a new area, we might just happen to see articles of interest or we might be able to connect them with somebody who is an expert in that field.

When people are launching a new business or product or a new service there may be many skills that they need to call on that they don't yet have. Very often it is **technical skills** or **marketing skills** or **help with PR,** so think about how can you help the people you know, how you can add value.

When you are **adding value** to them, you are **uppermost in their mind** and they will remember you, think of you warmly and also be keen to send business your way.

It's all about being **active in your business community** rather than just passively turning up to things, soaking up the information, absorbing the knowledge, meeting a few people and having a few interesting conversations.

When you are **giving back** you are contributing and you are seen then as one of the **key players** in that network, you are seen as one of the 'movers and shakers', somebody that they can rely on and who they can call on when they need a connection or advice.

If you are a speaker, you are one of the people who will be uppermost in their mind if they, or someone they know, wants someone **to speak at an event**.

TIP

25

Giving before we receive, is a really big part of **personal presence**. It is much more pleasurable and much more rewarding to give than it is to receive and when you do that, great things happen, doors open up, connections show up for you and the whole experience of being with, and networking with people becomes so much more exciting.

You get a **great buzz** when you have helped somebody and it's had a major impact on their business. You are then seen as a **major player** in their network, someone they trust implicitly and can refer with total confidence.

"Before giving, the mind of the giver is happy; while giving, the mind of the giver is made peaceful; and having given, the mind of the giver is uplifted." Buddha

TIP 26 – SUPPORTING OTHER PEOPLE'S EVENTS, A QUICK RE-CAP

It is so important on the networking circuit to not just be there to promote ourselves and sell our services, but to be thinking about how we can help others. This also applies when we are meeting with prospects and networking across social media.

It's not all "Sell, sell, sell, me, me, me", but actually "How can I help you?" I would like to carry on that theme of **giving before receiving** by talking about **supporting other people's events and special occasions** in their businesses.

These events happen all the time. If you are like me, you get invited to many book launches, to launches of new business offerings, to specific networking events people run from time to time and to charity events.

I try whenever I can, to **support my fellow networkers** when they are holding an event to attract people and draw attention to their service or product.

And **giving our time** is something that is really special. All of us have got limited working hours in every day. Our time is very precious, so to give up that time to be at an occasion or event that a colleague has organised, says a lot about our support for them.

So do try to fit those occasions in and when you do, **go the extra mile**, take somebody else with you, let your database know what is happening, where you are going, give them a reason to come to this event.

Is there a great speaker, is it a brilliant networking opportunity? Will they learn something new? If they sell products, is it a chance for them to display their goods,

When we start supporting our fellow networkers and colleagues, then of course they want to support us.

Again, that's not why we do it but it's that old **law of reciprocity**. 'What goes around comes around'.

When you are at the event, make the most of it, be one of those lovely people who mingles, who talks to strangers, who introduces people and brings a special kind of magic.

"Charismatic people have a special kind of magic that is truly irresistible"

Make other people feel at ease because at every event we go to, there will be people who are feeling nervous, who don't know many people and are just hoping that somebody talks to them. So be that lovely, warm, friendly person who is very happy to engage everyone and introduce them to key people that you know.

One of the things I always like to do when I have been to an event is to **email and thank the organiser**. Thank them for the time and effort they have put into the event, and if you can think of something specific that was really good about that event, then it makes it even more personal.

A lot of time and effort goes into arranging an event, not to mention nervous energy expended worrying about numbers and hoping all will go well. So there is nothing better and more reassuring afterwards than getting a flood of emails from grateful people telling you what a great job you have done.

So take a little bit of time to send a 'thank you', and share the success of the event across social media. Something like: "I have just been today to xxxxxx's book launch, what a brilliant book, what a great crowd of people!" or "I've just been to the launch of xxxxxx's new business, what an exciting new business, this is where you can find out more about it."

Add a **link to their website**. It's incredibly supportive and it only takes a few minutes to get other people's presence out across the social media that you use

Support others events, go the extra mile, take some guests, be fully present and promote on social media.

TIP

26

Doing this **raises your personal presence**, it shows that you care about other people, not just about yourself. It shows that you are a **big supporter of other people** and that you are inherently **invested in helping them succeed**.

What you get in return, is a network of happy, grateful people who are delighted to be in your circle!

> *"Some people give time, some money, some their skills and connections, some literally give their life's blood. But everyone has something to give."*
> *Barbara Bush*

TIP 27 – GIVING AWAY VALUE,
A QUICK RE-CAP

It is so good to support others – their functions, their networking events, their book and new business launches. At these events, it's even better when you are fully present, talking to other people and following up afterwards.

"We make a living by what we get; we make a life by what we give."
Winston Churchill

There is so much you can do to help others. I'm talking about **giving away value**. What I mean by this is **being prepared to give away some of your knowledge and expertise, without charging for it**.

That might sound rather strange as we are all in business ultimately to make money, we all have bills to pay. However, there are lots of ways in which we can give value to others and raise our profile, ways in which we can attract them to us but not necessarily charge them for it.

I've shared my personal presence tips on social media free of charge, because I just felt that I wanted to share some of my experience with building personal presence. It did not take me long to record the tips, and I was very happy to do it.

As a result of this I have had many comments on social media, people connecting with me, following me, and it's raised my personal presence across those media.

Think about how you can **share your expertise**, because we all have unique expertise in our own area and there are so many ways nowadays that you can share that knowledge. Just post on Facebook, share on LinkedIn, through your blog or as a guest blogger.

Guest Blogging is a great way to build a reputation with a group of people who don't know you.

When you are **guest blogging**, the best thing to do is to choose an **industry niche** that is specific for you, so the sort of people who are going to be reading that blog are the kind of people that are interested in your special subject.

Then write something **new, fresh and relevant** – make sure you include some latest facts, figures, statistics, quotes, whatever you can find, something that's **new** that Google will pick up on.
Google doesn't like regurgitated, 'same old' material, it picks up on anything new, and of course that all helps with the search engine rankings.

Blogging is an incredibly valuable tool to get yourself known and get your expertise out there to the masses.

If blogging is something you are not used to, or you blog very rarely or not at all, get some **proper advice**. Talk to somebody who is a regular blogger, or an expert on social media, and get some guidelines on it. That way you will be using your time wisely, your blog will be seen by the widest audience, you will get the right links out there for people to follow you and, in turn, you will find the right sites to guest blog on.

Think about **how you can share the value that you have**.
Not just blogging, but social media – LinkedIn, Twitter, Facebook etc.

You can give away an article, a downloadable pdf, a white paper or you can create an eBook quite easily. Anything that people will be willing to give their contact details for, so that you are building your database, and in return, they are getting great value from you.

It doesn't take a long time to do, short, punchy articles are read far more than long wordy ones. Writing gets you **seen and heard and remembered**, and of course, it shows you up as a **giver**, someone who is prepared to give something away expecting nothing in return.

TIP 27

Creating FREE value and get it out there across various media. Once you start doing that, it becomes habitual and every time you've got something new, you can share it. Your followers will build up, people will be talking about you, people will start to share your information and it will greatly increase your personal presence across all media.

"A generous man forgets what he gives and remembers what he receives." Old Proverb.

"We must not only give what we have; we must also give what we are."
Desire Joseph Mercier

TIP 28 – WHO DO YOU SPEND YOUR TIME WITH?

Harvey Mackay has written a wonderful book about networking, called – 'Dig Your Well Before You Are Thirsty'.

The premise of this book is we **shouldn't wait until we are desperate for business before we take action**.

We should be out there on the networking scene, even when we are really busy, building relationships, **maintaining** contact with our colleagues, clients and prospects and developing a **stronger personal presence** wherever we go!

Too many people decide to stop networking for a while, because they are so busy with tasks they have to do. Six months down the line, they suddenly find they haven't got a pipeline and they have lost touch with the people in their networks. Do follow Harvey's advice and even when you are busy, be out there on the networking scene.

It's interesting to watch people who are really busy and 'fired up' about their business. They are incredibly **attractive**, people are drawn to them because they want to understand why they are being so successful, they can sense their excitement and their passion for their business and they want to know more.

So when you are in that state, when you are really busy, enjoying what you are doing, stretched and challenged but rising to those challenges, **your personal presence is much higher.** People are naturally drawn to you, so it's a brilliant time to be out on the networking scene.

Harvey Mackay says that inspirational people **'drink at their wells of inspiration daily'** and what he means by that is that they surround themselves with other inspirational people. They surround themselves with **successful people**, people who are more successful than themselves, who will constantly challenge them and encourage them to move forward, to take bigger leaps, to try things they otherwise wouldn't try.

SO WHO DO YOU SPEND YOUR TIME WITH? I WANT YOU TO THINK ABOUT THAT.

Very often we hang on to connections and hang on to friendships and relationships because we feel that we have to, but actually more and more we find that the people we hang out with can drain our energy, they are not particularly interested in us, in our business, in our growth, in fact quite often they can feel **threatened** by it.

Some long-term friends may be slowing down or even not working any more. They might find it quite challenging to be with us if we are really excited and enthusiastic about our business. They are not going to give us the support we need, because they are not on the same wavelength.

So review who you spend your time with. I'm not suggesting you ditch all your life-long friends, but really think about **how much time** you are spending with people who **drain your energy** or who may try to hold you back. They are not doing this maliciously, but subconsciously. It's human nature. If they hold you back you will be more comfortable for them to be around.

Sometimes we can 'crave' that '**comfort zone**' – to be around people who expect nothing of us, and who even prefer it if we don't progress. However, if you are really serious about growing your business and taking yourself to the next level, spend time with **people who are going to take you there**.

The best people for you to spend time with are people who are:

- **Constantly growing** and **developing their own skills**
- **Trying things** that you have been scared to try
- **Taking themselves to the next level and beyond**

These are the sort of people who will **stimulate, motivate and inspire you to be the person you were born to be**

Of course, when you are fired up, inspired, motivated and challenging yourself, – you will become incredibly dynamic, energised and inspirational, and others will seek you out to spend time with you. .

Review who you are spending your time with, ask yourself whether they are inspiring you or draining your energy.
Then enjoy spending more time with all those wonderful, inspirational people who are genuinely supporting your continued success.

TIP
28

"Life is similar to a bus ride.
The journey begins when we board the bus.
We meet people along our way of which some are strangers, some friends and some strangers yet to be friends.
There are stops at intervals and people board in.
At times some of these people make their presence felt, leave an impact through their grace and beauty on us fellow passengers while on other occasions they remain indifferent.
But then it is important for some people to make an exit, to get down and walk the paths they were destined to because if people always made an entrance and never left either for the better or worse, then we would feel suffocated and confused like those people in the bus, the purpose of the journey would lose its essence and the journey altogether would neither be worthwhile nor smooth."
Chirag Tulsiani

TIP 29 – INVESTING IN YOU, A QUICK RE-CAP

It is so important to surround yourself with inspirational people, people who motivate you, challenge you and keep you moving forward towars your goals.

I'd like to continue that theme, by talking about **investing in you**. By this I mean planning your **future growth**, looking at your **goals** and your **vision**. Where do you want to get to, and what do you need to do to get yourself there? What do you need to learn, what new skills do you need to take on board, what experience do you need? What time do you need to put aside to plan your development?

It's incredibly easy when we are busy, particularly when we run our own business, to get so involved in the day to day tasks that we just put ourselves at the bottom of that 'to do' list and never get around to investing in ourselves.

Leaders of corporations invest in their own people and have regular training programmes in place so that staff are constantly adding to their skills. Very often, if you are a solopreneur or small business owner, you can forget to invest in your own **learning, development and growth**. Months and years can go past without us learning anything new other than what we learn through our mistakes.

Einstein said, *"If you feed your mind as often as you feed your stomach, then you'll never have to worry about feeding your stomach or a roof over your head or clothes on your back."*

So what I am suggesting you do, is really think about what **new skills** and what **new knowledge** would help you to achieve the goals you have set for yourself and the vision you have for your future.
Plan how you are going to attain these skills and that knowledge, put the dates in your diary. I recommend you invest **at least a full day every single**

month in your own **personal development**. It is an incredibly impactful practice to get into.

It will give you time to take stock of where you are, to re-evaluate where you are going. Sometimes this exercise can show you that you have got the ladder up against the wrong wall. You are continuing to climb that ladder but actually it is taking you to the wrong place. (Steven Covey)
Just **taking stock and taking time out** will make you see your business with **fresh eyes**.

Going on a **workshop or training course** will mean that once again you are spending time with other people who are inherently invested in developing themselves and in growing their business. You make some great new connections, you learn from the trainer, you learn from the other people in the room, from their experiences and of course, at the same time, you are building your network.

Invest in yourself and you will start
to **value** yourself more, because you are recognising that
you are your biggest asset and you are allowing
yourself time for your growth and development and your
self-esteem, confidence and personal presence will grow.

TIP
___
29

You can bring that **new knowledge** back to your business and to your network. You will have new information to share when you are at networking events, in your blogs, on social media and you suddenly grow in your area of expertise.

People listen to you because you have got something **new to share**. It positions you as an **'expert' in your field**.

Constant self-development is really important and of course as you know, when your confidence grows, when your knowledge grows, when your self-esteem grows then so does your personal presence.

Your **personal presence will be heard and seen more** because you have got more to talk about. And of course that added knowledge will take you closer to your **goals**.

So plan some time for you, time to invest in your biggest asset which is undoubtedly and absolutely – **YOU!**

> *"As human beings, our greatness lies not so much in being able to remake the world – that is the myth of the atomic age – as in being able to remake ourselves."*
> Mahatma Gandhi

TIP 30 – YOUR PERSONAL BRANDING STATEMENT

Do you have a strong personal branding statement?

This is a statement that **lets other people know what you are all about**. It should be the descriptor that comes after your name. So, your name tells them who you are and your personal branding statement tells them **what it is you do** and **what benefits you bring**.

So let me give you an example of that:-
On my marketing literature, my flyers, my business cards, you will see –

'Sylvia Baldock, Personal Presence and Team Dynamics Specialist, Unlocking the Hidden Potential in your Business'.

So, it says who I am, it says what I do and then it brings the benefit, which is unlocking that hidden potential.

Earlier on in this journey, we have looked at the **key words that describe you**.

What do people say about you? In their testimonials, what are the words that people use to describe you, what are the special attributes that you bring, that you offer?

Take a little time today to identify which of your **'key words' best describe you**, the sort of words people would use if they were telling somebody else about you and your services. These are the sorts of words people say in an email when they are following up after you have worked with them, delivered a service, spent some time with them, really helped them out, or perhaps they are words they have used in their emails to you.
Do they talk about your **energy**, your **inspiration**, your **depth of knowledge**? Your **Honesty, dependability, empathy**? What else do they

say? These are the key words we should be using in our marketing material, our emails, when we are writing those bios that people ask us to write if we are going to speak somewhere,
So really think about those key words today if you haven't done so already.

Make sure they are visible either on the wall of your office or, if you haven't got much room, photograph them and put them on your phone so you see them every time you open your phone up.

Also answer the questions -
- **What it is you do?**
- **What's special about you?**
- **What benefits do you bring**?
- **What do people say after you have worked with them?**

Write down some answers to the above questions and see which phrases resonate with you.

Now I actually spend some time working on this on my **Personal Presence Workshop**. I run these regularly and would be delighted if you could join me for a full day invested in you.

Remember **you are the biggest asset that you** and your business has and it's really important to **take regular time out to invest in that asset**.
It gives you time to make sure you are on track, re-evaluate where you are now and where you are going and get absolute clarity on the first steps you are going to take to get there.

We spend a whole day looking at you, your unique and special qualities, defining key words, giving you the **confidence** and the **words** to take away to make sure that you are **seen**, **heard** and **heard of**.

You can find **full details of my workshops here**
http://talent-dynamics.com/td/sylvia-baldock/
soon to be - www.sylviabaldock.com

Or email me on **sylvia.baldock@talent-dynamicsconsulting.com**

soon to be - sylvia@sylviabaldock.com

People leave my workshop feeling much more confident, with a much higher self-esteem and with much greater clarity about what is unique and special about them.

Testimonial from workshop attendee –

"The Personal Presence Day was fabulous for building confidence, re-connecting with your sense of purpose and allowing that to infuse through your whole being with the words and feelings that make you much more attractive to the clients you want to work with".
Helena Holrick

"The Personal Presence Day is a 'Must' for everyone. If business begins with a person, then what better way than to let it shine through that person? A journey of emotion and personal discovery that makes me feel I do have so much to offer". Jenna Haider

I hope you have enjoyed taking this journey, and that these tips will be useful as you develop and grow yourself and your business.

I invite you to continue the journey with me, **investing in yourself**, greatly **increasing your personal presence** and unlocking your hidden potential to be the person you were born to be.	**TIP** --- **30**

"Uniqueness is the individual gift that lies within each of us that wants to be expressed. The expression can only come alive through our physical experience. The ultimate purpose of our quest for happiness is to find a way to re-connect to that which makes us unique – this is our gift to ourself first and then to the world"
Aline Hanle The Quantum Catalyst

Copyright © Sylvia Baldock 2014-05-11

Sylvia Baldock, Personal Presence and Talent Dynamics Specialist and Trainer, Flow Consultant Trainer, Global Author, Public Speaker, Business/Personal Coach and Regional Director of The Athena Network.

A seasoned and engaging business trainer, coach and networking specialist who is passionate about empowering people to unlock the hidden potential in themselves and their business.

Through Talent Dynamics, Sylvia also offers a powerful business development pathway, which is having a major impact on individuals and companies world-wide.

Talent Dynamics profiling clarifies key strengths and challenges, enabling individuals and teams to play to their strengths and achieve far greater success and 'Flow' in their business and personal lives.

Sylvia is also passionate about 'Personal Presence' and runs workshops and webinars to enable people to establish a strong and impactful presence which makes them stand out from the crowd.

Delegates to these workshops re-discover their uniqueness, gain confidence and self-esteem, revisit their values, renew their vision and discover the words to share their uniqueness with others. In business, they attract their ideal clients and prospects – the people they really want to work with, doing the work they were born to do.

Sylvia inspires audiences regularly on the speaker circuit at conferences and events.

www.sylviabaldock.com

www.inspirationalspeaker.uk

www.linkedin.com/in/sylviabaldock

sylvia@sylviabaldock.com